P9-EKE-974

Mythical Beasts

by Doug Marx

CAPSTONE BOOKS

an imprint of Capstone Press
Mankato, Minnesota

MONTROSE LIBRARY DISTRI
320 So. 2nd St.
Montrose, CO 81401

Capstone Books are published by Capstone Press
151 Good Counsel Drive, P.O. Box 669, Mankato, Minnesota 56002
http://www.capstone-press.com

Copyright © 1991 Capstone Press. All rights reserved.
No part of this book may be reproduced without written permission from the publisher.
The publisher takes no responsibility for the use of any of the materials or methods
described in this book, nor for the products thereof.
Printed in the United States of America.

Library of Congress Cataloging-in-Publication Data
Marx, Doug.
    Mythical Beasts/by Doug Marx.
    p. cm.—(The Unexplained)
    Summary: Describes some of the mythical beasts that have existed in the
imaginations of people of all cultures throughout history. Includes Scylla, Minotaur,
griffin, phoenix, unicorn, and Bigfoot.
    ISBN 1-56065-046-X
    1. Animals, Mythical—Juvenile literature. 2. Monsters—Juvenile literature.
[1. Animals, Mythical. 2. Monsters.] I. Title. II. Series.
GR825.M22   1989
398.24'54—dc20   89-25201
                                                                    CIP
                                                                     AC

Photo/Illustration credits
The Children's Theatre Company, 6, 10, 20
Lisa Larson, 4, 8, 12, 14, 16, 18, 19, 22, 24, 26, 27, 30, 31, 34, 35, 44

2 3 4 5 6 04 03 02 01 00

Contents

The Ancient Past

Imagine you are living 3,000 years ago in ancient Greece. You and your family live in a tiny one-room cottage near some mountains. There are no highways, televisions, or items that use electricity. Many superhuman gods and goddesses live in the mountains near you. Wild animals also live there, including bears, wolves, hawks, and boars. They are dangerous. Not only can they run faster than humans, they also are better able to see and to smell. You live in close contact with wild and tame animals every day of your life. Your entire neighborhood is like a zoo, except that there are no cage bars to protect you. You know what it means to be afraid of the dark and the unknown.

At sundown, it gets pitch dark outside. Your family might have a fire inside. Nothing more. You are afraid of the dark. For a night's entertainment, you gather around the fire for a story. Your father tells of war and adventure. He tells of a brave Greek warrior named Odysseus (o-DIS-see-us), a leader in the Trojan War. By now the battle is over and Odysseus and his men are sailing home. On their way they must pass near a cliff where a horrible beast lives. In its cave, it waits for sailors.

The creature's name is Scylla (SIL-la) and it is the most terrible thing you have ever heard of. It has six snake's heads. Each head has rows of shark-like teeth. Its six

necks are scaly and long enough to reach down to snatch sailors right out of their ships. Also, six mean, barking dogs' heads are growing around its waist. Your eyes open wide as your father describes how this monster gobbles down six of Odysseus' men in "one" bite.

Scylla is a **mythical beast**. A mythical beast is an animal that lives only in the imagination. You believe that the Scylla exists. So do all of your ancient friends and neighbors. **Myths** are stories that tell of gods and other magical beings. They live in a world far different from our daily life.

Shape-Shifters

One of the interesting things about many mythical beasts is the way that they become what they are. **Shape-shifters** are mythical beasts that change from one form into another. Sometimes they change from an animal into a person. But, usually, they change from a person into an animal.

Today wolves are no longer the enemy of humankind that they were in other places and times. Think of what it was like to see wolf packs several hundred years ago, however, in the dark forests of Europe. Imagine them prowling around your cottage. Howling at the moon and

just waiting for a chance to eat your cow, one of your sheep – or maybe you. You are defenseless. Worse, the wolves escape every trap you set. They are so sly and cunning that they begin to seem immortal.

Pretend it is early evening. You are walking home. There are no streetlights on this road. Suddenly, the moon slips out from behind a cloud. In the moonlight, you see someone. The shadows make it look like he is holding his head and throat while shaking and trembling. The moonlight seems to work some dark magic on him. He starts changing. His clothes seem several sizes too small. His bones seem to stretch, his fingernails lengthen into claws. Hair sprouts all over his body. Foam forms around his teeth, which are now fangs.

When the wind roars, it sounds like a wolf howling. In your imagination, you think it is a real beast. You believe it is going to eat you. You say to yourself: "This can't happen." According to legend, you are not the first person to see a **werewolf**.

How much of this fear would it take to scare you into believing that a man or woman could turn into a supernatural wolf? Once people believed werewolves were humans who had made a pact with the devil or were possessed by demons. You might believe that it is hereditary. You and your friends are certain that were-

wolves are all over the place. You are suspicious of strangers or anyone with pointy ears, bushy eyebrows, or a relaxed way of walking. Because you believe werewolves are the work of the devil, you think they can be killed only by a silver bullet.

In ancient times, people had good reasons to fear the wild animals that lurked around their doors. It is not difficult to understand how these animals could become monsters in peoples' minds. Monsters such as werewolves, show us another side of human fear. Because werewolves are people who have changed, they show us how we fear ourselves. They show us how we fear our animal nature, that part of us that is still wild and untamed.

Not all shape-shifters are terrifying, though. In Northwest Native American tales, small boys regularly changed into otters. Eskimos claim that the raven is a superhuman being who could take the shape of a man or a bird. To the Eskimos, a raven created the world with all its animals and people.

Perhaps the gentlest of shape shifters, swan-maidens, appear wherever there are swans, particularly in India and Russia. The lovely swan-maidens – and many Native American mythical beasts, too – often reverse the werewolf tradition. In this myth, swans take the shape of beautiful women by taking off their gown of white

feathers when they go down to the lake to swim. According to legend, if a man is lucky enough to pass by when this happens, he can make such a beauty his wife.

Half Man, Half Animal

Shape-shifters tell us that humans and animals have some things in common. Many other ancient mythical beasts seem to be stuck. Half-human, half-animal, they don't change back and forth. These stories may show us something about the struggle to become fully human. The **Minotaur** (Min-ho-tor) is a famous example.

The Minotaur

According to the Minotaur myth, a king named Minos (My-nos) tricked Neptune, the god of the sea, into giving him a great white bull. Neptune did not like being tricked. He made the king's wife, Pasiphae (Pass-ih-fay), fall in love with the bull. One day Pasiphae gave birth to a gruesome creature that had the body of a man but the head of a bull. They called it Minotaur.

The Minotaur was a powerful monster. Steam flared from his nostrils. At night he shouted at the moon. The king locked the Minotaur in a labyrinth (lab-ber-rinth), which was a maze made of stone. All day the Minotaur

stormed through the damp, slimy labyrinths, unable to find his way out.

Every nine years, King Minos would force seven young men and seven young women to go down into the maze. They were sacrifices made to the Minotaur, who killed and ate them with delight.

One year, a brave Greek lad named Theseus (<u>Thee</u>-see-us) had to go down into the maze. The king's daughter, Ariadne (<u>Air</u>-ee-ad-nee), fell in love with Theseus. She gave him a ball of string, which he unwound as he wandered through the maze. No one knows exactly how Theseus killed the Minotaur, but he did. Theseus followed his yarn back to safety.

Centaurs

Centaurs (<u>sen</u>-tars) were half-stallion (or horse) and half-man. Centaurs lived in the mountains of Thessaly.

Most of the centaurs were rowdy creatures. Chiron (<u>sheer</u>-on), the most famous of all, was a wise and kindly beast. According to legend, he taught mankind the arts of healing, hunting, and music. He was a friend of Hercules, the strongest man in the world. One day, while Hercules was fighting with some mean centaurs, a poison arrow accidently struck Chiron.

Because Chiron was immortal, he could not die. But he could suffer enormous pain. He crawled off to a cave. Finally, a god took pity on this noble creature and lifted him up to the stars. It is said he became the constellation Sagittarius. Can you find the stars of Sagittarius in the night sky?

Satyrs

The ancient Greeks also believed in satyrs (<u>say</u>-ters). Satyrs were young men with the bodies of goats. They had bristly hair, pug noses, and pointy ears. For fun, they would scare shepherds and gentle Nymphs (Nimfs) who kept watch over the woodlands. Nymphs were young, beautiful female beings who protected flowers, birds, and children.

Of all the mythical beasts, none show how close we are to the animal world better than the "half-and-half" creatures. In India, there were men with beaks for noses and vulture's wings growing out of their shoulder blades. The great explorer Marco Polo claimed he saw dog-men on his journeys. Ancient Ireland was said to be inhabited by a warlike race of beasts called Formians. They were made up of all kinds of animals. Some were men with horses' heads. Others walked upright on flipper feet and had faces like men and fish.

An age-old mythological belief is that all forms of life have an *anima*, or soul. For thousands of years people believed that humans and animals had the same natures. Only their bodies were different. In other words, humans and animals shared the same soul. This makes it easier to understand how people could begin to believe in shapeshifters and "halfway" creatures.

Half Woman, Half Animal

There are also many half-woman, half-animal mythical creatures. This is fair, since one-half of the world's population is female.

Mermaids

Mermaids are the most beautiful and even-tempered of the female beasts. Most of the others, such as the Gorgons, are pretty nasty. A mermaid is a mythical creature whose top half is a beautiful woman and whose lower body is that of a fish. It is the most kind and gentle of the "half-woman, half-animal" beasts.

There are mermen, too, but because they haven't the same romantic appeal, we hardly even hear about them.

The beautiful mermaid in the movie *Splash* is another example of the way an ancient myth reappears in modern times.

Gorgons

Of the "half-woman, half-animal" beasts, Gorgons are the most destructive. Medusa (mee-<u>doo</u>-suh) is the best-known Gorgon. She was so ugly and grotesque that those who looked at her turned to stone. Her mouth had a pair of boar's tusks. Her thick, long red tongue swung forward and backward. Slimy scales covered her body. She had wings and her hands were like a vulture's claws – except made of brass. But, for all that, Medusa is best known for her hair. Her hair was a mass of hissing snakes.

Actually, Medusa was once a beautiful woman with golden hair. She made the mistake of falling in love with Poseidon (Poh-<u>sy</u>-dun), the god of the sea. Their love affair so angered the goddess Athena that she turned Medusa into a Gorgon.

Eventually, the Greek hero, Perseus (<u>Per</u>-see-us), killed Medusa by chopping off her head. He snuck up on her while she slept. He was not turned to stone because he looked only at the image of Medusa that was reflected in his shiny shield.

That is not the end of the story, however. At the very moment that Perseus was killing Medusa, she gave birth to a couple of "children." They bubbled up out of the blood. One was Pegasus, the exquisite winged-horse. The other was the monster Chrysao, the father of the monsters **Geryon** and **Echidna**.

Echidna

Echidna (Ek-id-nuh) is another half-woman, half-animal mythical beast. Sometimes she is called a "witch-adder." She had a woman's head and serpent's body. After robbing people, she would crush them to death by coiling around them. Echidna gave birth to yet another, this one called the Hydra. Initially, the Hydra had nine serpent's heads, but since every time somebody cut one off two more would grow back, it was hard to keep count of her heads.

Echidna, who bore several monsters, also gave birth to another "daughter" called the Sphinx. There is a likeness of a Sphinx in the form of a monument among the Pyramids of Egypt, except the Egyptian statue has the head of a man. The original Sphinx had a woman's head, a lion's body, a serpent's tail, and the wings of an eagle. She asked riddles of all the young men who would pass by her perch. If they could not answer correctly, she would eat them on the spot.

Combination Mythical Beasts

If you think the shape-shifters and half-human, half-animal creatures are strange, consider the Chimera (<u>Kim</u>-er-uh). The Chimera had the head and forelegs of a ferocious lion. A goat's head grew from its back. Its tail was a fanged snake. The Chimera was a female monster. She had another pair of scaly legs that made her amazingly quick. Flames shot from her lion's head. Venom spewed from her snake's head. The long-toothed goat hissed and screamed. Homer, an ancient Greek poet, wrote that the Chimera destroyed the land of Lycia.

Remember Pegasus, the winged horse that was born when Perseus killed Medusa? Pegasus (<u>Peg</u>-uhses) – who is also a "combination animal" – shows us that good things can come from bad.

As it happens, if not for Pegasus, the Chimera might still be alive today. The Chimera lived high in the mountains above a blackened wasteland. Vultures glided overhead. The land around smelled of rotting, burning flesh. Only birds could get close to the Chimera.

A young man named Bellerophen (Bel-air-oh-fon) attempted to slay the beast. He figured his only chance was to catch Pegasus and fly to the monster's perch on a cliff. Dodging flames and poison, Pegasus circled the beast. Bellerophen shot arrow after arrow until the Chimera lay dead.

Creatures of Flight

The sky is a special place. It is the home of the stars, the sun, and the moon. Whether we call it Heaven, or "the last frontier," the human imagination runs free there. Also, it is the element in which birds fly. Probably nothing has obsessed human beings so much as the desire to fly like a bird.

Little wonder, then, that the mythical beasts of the air should be among the most beautiful and poetical. Except for the griffin – which is part mammal, and the Cockatrice, which could not fly – most creatures of the air express hope and rebirth. They are symbols of the best human dreams. We have already mentioned the Raven, which the Eskimos believe created the world with all its animals and people. But what of the dove that saved Noah and his ark full of animals?

Cockatrice

The Cockatrice is one of the scariest mythical beasts. Its story originated during the Middle Ages. It was a creature with no mother, born of a yokeless egg laid by a rooster.

A toad was said to have hatched it on a dunghill. What popped out was a vicious giant rooster with leathery wings.

One of the wickedest beasts ever, the Cockatrice had such bad breath that a whiff of it set people on fire. Its hiss alone paralyzed those nearby. Oddly, carrying a mirror was said to be one of the ways to protect oneself against it. This creepy rooster-serpent was so horrible that it would drop dead when it saw is own reflection.

Griffins

Another monster of flight is the **griffin**. There's one in the story *Alice in Wonderland*. Unlike Alice's friendly monster, however, most griffins weren't at all kind.

The front half of the griffin was a monstrous eagle. The back half was a lion. The griffin liked to swoop down to steal the gold men dug out of the mines. When no treasure was available, it often settled for a man instead.

In the Middle Ages, people believed that if a griffin's claw could be used as a drinking cup, it would change color if the drink in it had been poisoned. But since nobody had really seen a griffin, antelope's horns were used instead.

Phoenix

Another mythical bird is the Phoenix (<u>Fee</u>-nix). Birds were often associated with the sun and moon. The Phoenix myth first appeared in Egypt and the Middle East. Ancient Egyptians believed the Phoenix lived in Paradise, which lay beyond the eastern horizon where the sun comes up every morning.

The Phoenix was the most beautiful of all birds. Larger than an eagle, it had a golden head. Its feathers held all the colors of fire – reds, purples, gold and blue. Legend tells us that the Phoenix lived in Paradise for 1,000 years until it became tired and the time came for it to die. But it couldn't die in Paradise, so it flew westward, just as the sun does each day. At night, it built a nest in a palm tree.

At dawn, the Phoenix sang the sun into flight. As the first rays of the sun touched the tips of the highest palms, the nest exploded into flames. The fire smelled of cinnamon and sweet spices. When there was nothing left of the Phoenix but ashes, the ashes began to stir. And, behold! Out of the ashes came a new bird, which flew back to Paradise to live another 1,000 years.

Other cultures around the world have mythical birds much like the Phoenix. The Chinese believe in **Feng-huang** (Feng-wang). Feng-huang is a cross between a pheasant and a peacock. Its feathers were radiant with all the light

MONTROSE LIBRARY DISTRICT
320 So. 2nd St.
Montrose, CO 81401

of Paradise. Whenever Feng-huang appeared in the sky, the Chinese believed they would enjoy many years of peace and prosperity.

The Russian Firebird is another example. It had eyes like crystals and wings like flames. A single feather would bring light to the darkness. The Phoenix, Feng-huang, and the Firebird show us how birds were believed to be masters of darkness. Belief in them helped people overcome their fear of death, misfortune, and the spooky night world.

Beasts of the Waters

Like the sky, the sea holds a special place in the human imagination. Vast and mysterious, it is a frontier human-kind has yet to fully explore. Strange, often huge, creatures live in the sea. Whales, giant squids, swordfish, jellyfish – these animals must have seemed like monsters to ancient sailors. Some people believe that the mermaid myth began when a sailor saw a sea lion basking in the sun on a distant shoreline. Also, the sea is often thought of as a symbol for the depths of the human mind.

Beasts such as the Hydra and Minotaur symbolize our inner fears and temptations. (Was the nine-headed Hydra really an eight-legged giant octopus with its head in the middle?) Monsters are strange messages sent from within our minds. They also symbolize possibility. The ocean and the human imagination are places where all kinds of life forms live.

The oldest of these creatures is probably the sea serpent. It is snake-like and may have to do with peoples' fear of pythons and eels. The interesting thing about sea serpents is that we still partly believe in their existence. Scientific knowledge during the last two centuries has made us skeptical of mythical beasts. However, we don't know that much about the depths of the sea. Sometimes, even today, a fisherman will net a fish that we thought had died out in the age of the dinosaurs. Maybe a huge serpent is still alive down there, hidden from our eyes.

Probably the largest of these mythical beasts of the sea was known to the people of Norway as the Kraken (Krayken). It measured a mile and a half in circumference! The Kraken was so big that sailors often mistook it for an island. Imagine their surprise when they landed on it and built campfires for the night.

Not all sea monster stories have died out. Have you ever heard of Scotland's Loch Ness Monster? Many people claim to have seen "Nessie" since the turn of the century. First reported in a local newspaper, the monster became a worldwide story. Newspapers and television have made "Nessie" a household word. Sometimes blurry snapshots

are offered as proof of its existence. Is "Nessie" just a curious seal that swam up the river Ness and got trapped in the lake for a while? Or just a tree trunk floating on the surface? We may never know for sure. Still, "Nessie" shows us how easily a mythical beast can be born even in our own time.

Big-Time Beasts

Unicorns

Birds chirp, butterflies zig-zag, and a clear stream gurgles through a forest. Yellow sunlight shines lime-green in the leaves. A beautiful maiden in a flowing white dress sits under a tree.

Suddenly, a magnificent white horse with a single horn appears. It approaches the maiden, puts its head in her lap, and falls asleep.

But hunters with dogs and spears appear out of no-where, surrounding the beautiful horse. It rears and kicks, but to no use. A spear enters its heart and the animal dies. The hunters cut off its horn and leave the carcass to rot.

This is the story most often told about **unicorns**. Of all the mythical beasts, none were as magical and enchanting

as unicorns. Stories about the graceful, marvelous creatures were told from Europe to China. Unicorns mentioned as long as 2,500 years ago were described as having the feet of an elephant and the head of a boar. Most commonly, however, unicorns are described as shining white horses with a single horn growing from their foreheads.

They were said to be able to fly, making in flight the ringing sound of a beautiful bell. Symbols of purity and justice, unicorns were thought to live deep within wilderness forests, safe from humankind. They could be ferocious when attacked. But usually they were described as gentle, noble beasts with no desire to harm any creature.

Dragons

Dragons are probably the most popular of all mythical beasts. They are giant reptiles with long wings and forked, snaky tongues. Dragons were said to live in caves and deep holes in the ground, guarding gold. Still other types of dragons were thought to inhabit the sky and sea. Many dragons were mean. Others were gentle and shy. In some cultures, dragons are symbols of evil. In other cultures, they are symbols of good. The dragons we are most familiar with shoot flames from their mouths. There were also said to be dragons with a breath so sweet they could lure birds into their mouths.

In the Western world dragons were thought of as sinister creatures. The Western dragon's aim in life was to poison human souls. Because the dragon was looked on as so hideous, legends tell the stories of the heroes who came to kill it. In this way, the dragon myth was like that of Bellerophon and the Chimera. Dragons are also thought to be related to the Cockatrice myth.

In Asia, or the Eastern world, just the opposite is true. There the dragon is a symbol of wisdom and good fortune. It brings the spring rains at planting time. It ensures that the rivers do not flood and the wind does not blow too hard. When the dragon flies to heaven, the pressure of its feet on the clouds makes rain. If a dragon gets angry, a storm will follow. In Chinese mythology, dragons are often shape-shifters. They live in the sea and appear on land as brave kings.

Sometimes myth and reality draw very close together. Would you believe that on the island of Komodo in the East Indies, there lives a real dragon? It is called the Komodo Dragon. It eats meat and has been known to kill humans. It is actually a lizard that grows to a length of 12 feet. The Komodo Dragon was "discovered" in 1912.

Mythical Beasts: Do We Have Them Today?

From sea serpents and dragons, we can see that mythical beasts are very close to us. In fact, they are so close, our movie monsters are often based on our images of the monsters of old. A mythical beast isn't necessarily old. We have mythical beasts of our own today. Instead of listening to monster stories by the light of a campfire, we go see a movie.

Imagine the terrifying creature in the movie *Alien*. It is a huge lizard with a long tail and shiny scales, chemical acid for blood, and rows of stainless steel teeth. As it happens, the *Alien* Beast is just like Scylla. It even eats six of the crew – just like Scylla did. So, though the beasts we see in movies might seem brand new, most are modeled on mythological animals of the past.

Are there other beasts we could call mythical in our own time? How about the furry Ewoks, the loyal companion of the *Star Wars* crew? The weird "animals" encountered by the starship Enterprise as it journeys through distant galaxies in *Star Trek* are also our modern mythical beasts.

The mermaid in Splash is like the historical image we have of her. Our idea of what beasts look like has not

changed much – whether ugly or beautiful. However, what we think about them has changed. The mythical beasts of the past were thought to be creations of the gods. They were simply creatures, beyond human control. Today, the beasts in movies and fantasy books are created by the actions of men.

Beasts We Still Believe In

Whether they be ancient or modern, mythical beasts are now known to be imaginary. However, there are beasts many people still believe in.

Since the beginning of the 20th century, a beast called the **yeti** (yeh-tee) has been rumored to exist in the Himalayan mountain range. A "halfway" creature, the yeti is also known as the "Abominable Snowman." For many years, explorers climbing these high, remote mountains have reported finding huge footprints in the snow. The explorers were told by people who live in the mountains that the footprints were made by a giant, hairy, ape-like beast with a human face. Its arms are said to reach to its knees. Yeti are supposed to live in caves high on the remote slopes of the Himalayas. The yeti is so strong it is said to be able to uproot trees and lift boulders.

Some say the yeti will attack and eat humans. Others insist it is shy and harmless. The yeti, or Abominable Snowman, might be real. Some people have formed clubs around the world to continue the search for this beast. They publish maps and other information on the most recent sightings.

At any rate, the only evidence we have of the yeti are fuzzy photographs and footprints, which might be fake. North and South Americans also have their own version of the yeti called Sasquatch, or "Big Foot." There are several Sasquatch clubs, too. A recent movie, *Harry and the Hendersons*, is about one of these beasts. Sasquatches have been reportedly seen all over the United States and Canada.

These creatures might be made up (mythical), but – they might be real. Anthropologists have discovered the bones of an ape-like creature that lived six to nine million years ago in China and India. This ape stood eight to nine feet tall and weighed about 600 pounds! Because of its size, this creature was named Gigantopithecus (Jy-<u>gant</u>-oh-<u>pith</u>-ih-kus). Gigantopithecus is believed to be extinct, but it looked just like people claim Bigfoot does.

Is Bigfoot really Gigantopithecus? It would not be the first time that a mythical beast turned out to be genuine. Gorillas, mammoths, tapirs, and lizards the size of dragons were also treated with skepticism when first heard of by Westerners.

Glossary

Centaurs: Half-stallion and half-man.

Echidna: A half-woman, half-animal beast.

Feng-huang: A bird that is a cross between a pheasant and a peacock.

Geryn: A winged, three bodied monster.

Griffin: A beast with the body and hind legs of a lion and the head and wings of a monstrous eagle.

Minotaur: A monster with a body of a man and the head of a bull.

Mythical beasts: Strange and unusual creatures used in myths.

Myths: Stories of fiction with unknown origin used to explain phenomenons of nature, origin of man, customs, religious beliefs, etc.

Shape shifters: Mythical beasts that can change from one form into another.

Unicorn: A horselike creature with a single horn growing in the center of its forehead.

Werewolf: A human that turns into a supernatural wolf.

Yeti: A large creature covered with hair that is believed to be living in the Himalayan Mountains.